KETTLEBELL

The Ultimate Kettlebell Workout to Get Shredded

(The Beginner's and Advance Guide to Kettlebells)

Shirley Evans

Published by Tomas Edwards

© **Shirley Evans**

All Rights Reserved

Kettlebell: The Ultimate Kettlebell Workout to Get Shredded (The Beginner's and Advance Guide to Kettlebells)

ISBN 978-1-990268-65-6

All rights reserved. No part of this guide may be reproduced in any form without permission in writing from the publisher except in the case of brief quotations embodied in critical articles or reviews.

Legal & Disclaimer

The information contained in this book is not designed to replace or take the place of any form of medicine or professional medical advice. The information in this book has been provided for educational and entertainment purposes only.

The information contained in this book has been compiled from sources deemed reliable, and it is accurate to the best of the Author's knowledge; however, the Author cannot guarantee its accuracy and validity and cannot be held liable for any errors or omissions. Changes are periodically made to this book. You must consult your doctor or get professional medical advice before using any of the suggested remedies, techniques, or information in this book.

Upon using the information contained in this book, you agree to hold harmless the Author from and against any damages, costs, and expenses, including any legal fees potentially resulting from the application of any of the information provided by this guide. This disclaimer applies to any damages or injury caused by the use and application, whether directly or indirectly, of any advice or information presented, whether for breach of contract, tort, negligence, personal injury, criminal intent, or under any other cause of action.

You agree to accept all risks of using the information presented inside this book. You need to consult a professional medical practitioner in order to ensure you are both able and healthy enough to participate in this program.

Table of Contents

INTRODUCTION 1

CHAPTER 1: SHOULDERS AND ARMS 4

CHAPTER 2: SELECTING KETTLEBELLS.............................. 12

CHAPTER 3: TYPES OF KETTLEBELLS................................ 17

CHAPTER 4: THE BENEFITS OF KETTLEBELL TRAINING 23

CHAPTER 5: KETTLEBELL TRAINING................................. 34

CHAPTER 6: RUSSIAN KETTLEBELL SWING 44

CHAPTER 7: COMBO EXERCISES (UPPER AND LOWER BODY).. 49

CHAPTER 8: HIGH INTENSITY INTERVAL TRAINING 51

CHAPTER 9: PREPARING FOR YOUR KETTLEBELL WORKOUT 54

CHAPTER 10: THE 8 WEEK TRAINING PLAN 58

CHAPTER 11: RULES FOR STRUCTURING WORKOUTS 87

CHAPTER 12: PERSONALIZE IT! 102

CONCLUSION 115

Introduction

Kettlebells have become a gym staple today because of the unlimited training opportunities they offer. A kettlebell is a type of dumbbell except that the weight is not distributed evenly in a kettlebell. Kettlebells are shaped like a ball that comes with a handle to provide an easy grip. Kettlebells can range from 5 pounds to over 100 pounds in weight.

Kettlebell training has become a popular method to lose weight, build strength, improve balance, maintain fitness, and get a toned and beautiful body. Kettlebell training has now become a part of most of the weight loss programs because it is a time-saving calorie burning solution. According to the American Council on Exercise (ACE), an average person can burn 400 calories in just twenty minutes by doing kettlebell exercises.

The origin of kettlebells is still a matter of speculation. The word 'Girya' meaning kettlebell was first published in the Russian dictionary in the early eighteenth century. Kettlebells became popular in the West in the late twentieth century when a Soviet physical training instructor wrote an article on Kettlebells in a popular American magazine.

There are many different weight loss exercises that can be done with kettlebells. Some of the most popular ones include the following:

1. Air squat
2. Kettlebell deadlift
3. Kettlebell goblet squat
4. Kettlebell two-handed swing
5. Kettlebell one-handed swing

Some of these exercises require high degree of training and skill. If not done properly, kettlebell exercises may provide little benefit and can result in serious injuries. Guidance by a qualified trainer can help the user in having a safe and effective experience of kettlebell exercises.

Chapter 1: Shoulders And Arms

When starting kettlebell training, you should begin with kettlebell exercises that deal with mainly the shoulders and arms. The exercises listed below, though they may affect different muscle groups, affect mainly the shoulders and the arms. Most are simple to learn and master, some may need some expertise before they can be mastered, but all are sure to provide benefits that most conventional training methods will find to mirror.

1. The Kettlebell Slingshot

Target muscle group: Shoulders, Arms

Walkthrough: This fluid type exercise is quite easy to do on paper, but it is trickier to learn and master than it looks, and can take hours of practice to perfect. The immediate benefits of this exercise may not be evident, but as time progresses, you will realize that the flexibility in your shoulders has improved, and that strength in the arms has increased.

You start off by standing straight, with your feet shoulder length apart. Hold the kettlebell in front of your body at about chest level and swing the weight behind your back. With your other hand, reach behind your back and grab the weight, bringing it full circle back to your chest. This counts as one rep. Upon completion of one set, reverse the direction of the swing and repeat the exercise. This is a fantastic exercise for your whole upper body as the motion involved with swinging the kettlebell around you engages more than just the shoulder and arm muscles. This routine can also do a world of good for both your core and your obliques, with your chest and back also benefiting from the swinging movement.

2. The Kettlebell Military Press

Target muscle group: Shoulders, arms and back

Walkthrough: This is one of those drills that can be done quite easily by using more conventional dumbbells, but is more effective when using kettlebells. The weight distribution on a kettlebell ensures that you have to pay more attention to the way the weight behaves as you are doing the press. This helps to guarantee that you get more out of the workout as you have to concentrate more to make sure that the weight is working to your advantage.

As this is very much like the standard dumbbell military press, to begin with, grab a kettlebell and clean it up to the rack position (the clean exercise shall be explored more later on in this book). The rack position is a position where the kettlebell is held in your hand, elbow bent, with your fist close to your chest, while the weight rests lightly on your forearm close to your body. From the rack position, press the weight straight up while leaning forward slightly. This will ensure that the weight of the kettlebell is positioned behind your head. Bring the weight down and back into the rack position to complete one rep. Switch arms at the end of the set and repeat the exercise. If you like an extra challenge, this set can be done with two kettlebells at the same time.

3. Kettlebell Pirate Ships

Target muscle group: Shoulders, Arms, Back

Walkthrough: One of those very aptly named exercises, this drill is unique because after doing a few of these reps, you will understand why they were called pirate ships. This particular exercise is excellent for building up the strength in your shoulders, as well as your arms, back and obliques as it engages your complete upper body during execution.

To begin with, start with your feet just a bit wider than shoulder length apart. Hold the kettlebell with both hands, and let the weight hang at waist level, with your arms fully extended. Start the exercise by swinging the kettlebell in one direction, to about head height, while twisting your body in the same direction, keeping your eyes on the weight all the time.

Hold the weight at head high for a second or two before allowing it to drop. As it drops, twist your body in the other direction, and let the weight follow your body in a pendulum like movement. Again, lift it up to head height and hold it there for a second or two before letting the weight drop back down to the starting position. Count this as one rep. This exercise should be done both in the conventional 3 to 5 sets work out, but can also be done as a time trial, to see not only how long you can go, but also how many reps you can do before your body gets tired.

4. Kettlebell High Pull

Target muscle group: Shoulders, Arms

Walkthrough: This is a fluid style exercise that is extremely useful to learn and master, though it may not be as easy as it seems. When described and demonstrated, the high pull seems like an easy enough routine to master, but the proper form and body positions are hard to pull off properly. Appropriate supervision the first few times this is done is recommended, especially for first timers, just to ensure that form is held properly throughout the workout.

To begin, place your feet shoulder length apart and point your toes outwards at a forty-five degree angle. Place the kettlebell on the ground between both legs and squat towards it, keeping your back straight in the process. Grab the kettlebell with one hand and rise back up to the starting position, pulling the kettlebell up with your arm to about shoulder level. Lower the weight back down and repeat the process with your other arm to complete one rep.

This one-arm high pull has been described as a transition move, just like the kettlebell clean, as it is a part of the movement that is used to achieve the kettlebell snatch.

5. The Kettlebell Figure 8

Target muscle group: Arms, Shoulders

Walkthrough: This is a perfect example of a crossfit inspired Kettlebell exercise. The figure 8 maneuver was popularized by the street basketball world before it became evident how beneficial this repeated movement was to the development of muscles in the arms and shoulders. As well as this, it was also noticed that a happy side effect of this was the strengthening of the lower back muscles, though this is not as evident as the growth that is witnessed in the shoulders and arms of people who do this exercise.

To execute the figure 8 with a kettlebell, first place both feet a little wider than hip width apart and lower your body into the squat position, ensuring that you keep your back straight. Grab the kettlebell with your left hand, and pass it through the outside of the left leg, passing it back between the legs to your right hand. Mirror the just concluded process with your right hand to complete one rep. Though you can do 10 to 15 reps as recommended; with this exercise, every once in a while you can try a time trial to see just how long you can go. This is a particularly good crossfit workout for those looking to strengthen particularly their arms and lower back.

There are many more exercises that focus on the arms and shoulders, but these are some of the most effective of all. With a few sessions of practice, these exercises are sure to become part of your regular training regimen; and with time, a rather shorter time than normal, the benefits of these workouts will shine through.

Chapter 2: Selecting Kettlebells

Kettlebells are weights with a round shape, made of cast iron, and with an attached handle so users can get hold of them without difficulty. These items have been around for decades but became popular once more only recently. Users have found that one very unique quality of this equipment is that it allows you to use dynamic movements to develop strength, endurance, agility, and balance. Many have become fond of using it because it is effective, challenging, and very handy. It is held with one hand or both while doing different swings, pulls, and presses.

There are moves that require for the weight to be transferred from one hand to the other while the weight is moved upwards or the holder moves in a lateral motion. These necessitate that the person balances his body and works his abdominal muscles in a way different than usual. Other movements make use of power or strength that comes from the hips and the lower extremities. This facilitates the movement of the weight providing the body with combined bodily actions that are usually not included in other forms of training exercises.

Difference between kettlebells and dumbbells

Some people may think that the kettlebell is a type of dumbbell, but it is not. In certain aspects, they may be similar but the kettlebell has a distinctive shape. It may appear like a typical weight; however, its u-shaped handle affects the way the weight develops the body. Since the center of mass for a kettlebell is outside the hand, it can be shifted contingent on the way it is held and moved. It is not the same with dumbbells wherein the center of gravity always lies in the hand of the user.

Kettlebell movements generate a centrifugal force concentrating more on the decelerating and stabilizing muscles.

This is not the applied concept on long-established strength training programs. The type of movement using kettlebells involve multiple directions which people find themselves doing in their activities of daily living. One example is when a person carries a small travel case to be placed in a compartment above the head. More examples include lifting overstuffed luggage or a grocery bag with lots of stuff.

When kettlebells are used regularly, they can provide almost the same benefit in terms of functional and actual strength. Dumbbells facilitate the building of muscle strength by applying slow and restrained movements. On the other hand, the kettlebell training makes use of the whole body and concentrates on developing power, dynamic moves, and staying power. The distinct shape of the kettlebell allows for a smooth shift from one exercise to another without having to place the equipment on the floor. This non-stop technique or "kettlebell flow" is known to result to greater metabolic burn and development of more muscle in considerably less time.

Guidelines for choosing weights

Kettlebells have various designs and weights that start from five pounds and heavier with five-pound increments up to more than a hundred pounds. In selecting the appropriate weight, make certain it is heavy enough but will not be too strenuous for your workout. Ascertaining the proper weight may be a bit tricky at first but eventually, you will realize that every kettlebell activity has a load requirement. For beginners, a lot of the ballistic movements like push press and swing may seem new and awkward; hence, instructors recommend to begin with light weights to master the form first.

Suggested guidelines for selecting your weight:

5 to 10 lbs for women who are only starting to train

10 to 15 lbs for women who know about kettlebell workouts or for men who are beginners

20 to 25 lbs for women who have previous experience with this training or for men who have knowledge about kettlebell training

30 lbs and up for those who are fit enough and have tried kettlebell workouts before

For individuals who want to engage in this training on a regular basis, it requires different weights contingent to the type of exercise to be performed. If unsure, begin with light weight exercises and get familiarized with the movements before deciding to use a heavier weight. These items may be purchased in many sporting goods outlets as well as online providers. They may be costly but these can be used for strength training workouts also.

Chapter 3: Types Of Kettlebells

There are different types of kettlebells. The most popular types are powder coat kettlebell, cast iron kettlebell, and steel competition kettlebell

Powder coat kettlebell

The difference between powder cast kettlebell and cast iron kettlebell is the powder coating which makes it more durable. The colored bands on the handles indicate weight.

Cast iron kettlebell

They are commonly used for muscle building. They have thick smooth handles optimized to prevent chafing. They have a flat base for easy storage. The kettlebells are stamped in kilograms and their sizes depend on weight. Exercising using these kettlebells, depend on an individual and how much one wants to challenge the shoulders.

Steel competition kettlebells

They are all of the same sizes regardless of weight hence any weight will always fit in your hands in the same exact way. They are color coded to international standards.

Rubber coated kettlebells as their name suggests are coated with rubber and do not undergo rust.they also don't scratch. They come in different sizes depending on weight.

Vinyl kettlebells are coated with vinyl a synthetic resin comprising of different colors that give it a sophisticated appeal.

Classic kettlebells increase in size as the corresponding weight increases. A 50kg kettlebell is bigger than a 10 kg kettlebell.

Lifting Techniques

The following techniques detail the correct form and how to go about common kettlebell exercises. If you are new to kettlebell training it is recommended that you get a partner or coach who is familiar with the exercises as an incorrect form can lead to back pains. This happens when there is an intense amount of stress placed on the posterior chain when doing the swings. Working with kettlebells requires a combination of proper form and an understanding of the correct posture, grip balance, and transitions. Just like with other exercises equipment it is important to learn how to correctly use the kettlebells to avoid injuries and to ensure a successful workout plan. There are excellent DVDs available to help train one with the proper handling techniques of kettlebells but one would still need to work with a certified instructor in order to get the right moves and perform them safely.

Style

There are three different styles of lifting kettlebell which all bring slightly different results.

Hard style. This is said to be the original kettlebell workout and involves generating explosive power and strength. Kime technique is the principle behind hard style and is an all-out effort in every repetition. The aim is to produce the power needed to swing, snatch, press or squat but increasing power is key. This style utilizes fast rigid movements as opposed to smooth and fluid motions. For this reason, it is also called the Russian kettlebell challenge. Hard styles maximize both extremes in terms of tension and strength while still concentrating on relaxation and speed. The tenser the muscle the more the force produced. They increase strength by contacting muscles harder. Each workout produces more output but in less time.

Sports style. This style combines power and strength for overall endurance. It requires an athlete to work under a sub maximal load, lifting the kettlebell as many times as possible in a set time frame of ten minutes.

Juggling. It is insane to conceptualize the idea of one juggling a steel ball weighing 10 or20 pounds but it has already become a very popular style of kettlebell lifting. It provides increased ability in core strength and resistance to rotation. It also enhances hand-eye coordination and brings powerful pulling strength and above all its fun.

HOLDS

A kettlebell can be held in different ways to achieve a range of the required results. The way you hold, grip, grab and the angle determines the muscle to be used and the difficulty to be endured. Using one hand or both during a workout also affects the result.

Racked. In this position, the arm is bent with the upper arm held tight to the body and the hand in line with the chin. The handle is in your palm and the bell is on the outside.

By the horns. This is a common position for beginners and involves holding the kettlebell by the horns. The bell is held close to the chest.

Squeeze or crush. This is almost similar to by the horns but instead of gripping by the horns you hold the bell by squeezing it with the base of your fingers. The lack of grip makes it necessary for the arm muscles to compensate.

Waiter. The kettlebell is made to rest in your open palm.

POSTURE

When exercising with kettlebell it is very important to maintain the appropriate posture so as to prevent injury. Primary consideration should be made to avoid hunching forward with rounded shoulders. The head should face forward with the eyes focused roughly 6 feet ahead down. The spine should retain its natural S curve. This position makes you look like you are just about to sit down on a chair. In this position, you should be able to place a stick along your spine from your head to your hips with contacts with the head shoulders and upper glutes.

Chapter 4: The Benefits Of Kettlebell Training

There are so many benefits that you get to enjoy by performing kettlebell workouts. One thing that is important to note is that kettlebell training offers a unique combination of benefits from strength exercises and cardio. As mentioned earlier, kettlebell workout is more unconventional and quite resembles a cannonball with a handle attached to it. You can use it to build your strength, agility, boost balance and endurance while at the same time burn fat.

Kettlebell exercises often feature a wide range of lifts and swings. The good thing is that the training tool is quite flexible and can be used for a broad range of intense training exercises. Therefore, if you need a hybrid system for both strength and cardio, the kettlebells are your best option at creating workouts that are not only effective but also time efficient.

So, if you are still weighing whether or not to ditch those conventional dumbbells for something that will be worth your while, here are some of the benefits that you do not want to miss when you choose the kettlebell training;

1. Achieve Better Form

One of the main things that distinguish a kettlebell from a d usually lies on the offset nature of the load. This is mainly because the center of gravity of a kettlebell is about 6-8 inches away from your grip when you are holding the handle, and this is what makes it quite difficult to control.

Because of this, every exercise that you perform ranging from convenutal strength movements to more unique kettlebell exercises such as swings, you are going to need a strict form and increased activation of the muscles than you could get from using dumbbell.

Let us consider an overhead press. In this case, one of the funniest things when using dumbbell is the fact that so many people are just as happy to press at the point where their elbows are bent at a right angle. However, with kettlebell, the first

instinct is to press up to lockout. This is mainly because the offset load serves as a counterweight that plays a critical role in pulling the shoulders back.

In other words, the kettlebell plays a significant role in encouraging you to perform each exercise optimally and perfectly. However, if you cannot, for instance, you end up arching your back or twisting to one side when trying to complete the lift, then you most certainly know that your form is broken.

When you squat with the kettlebell held in front of your body, this causes you to sit back, and this improves the mechanics of your squat patter tremendously. This in effect paves the way for you to progress to more advanced exercises seamlessly when you get stronger.

2. Improves Core Strength

When you press a kettlebell overhead, you are simply causing your ribs and back to flare. This means that you have to lock your core as much as possible to balance your posture. When you are in a swing, it is critical that you brace your core to prevent your lower back from dangerously rounding at the bottom of the

movements. Therefore, for each exercise you perform, the good thing is that you can count on your core firing harder with the aim of stabilizing your body and ensuring that your safety comes first.

3. Boost Athleticism

If you are an athlete, one of the major benefits of incorporating kettlebells in your workout routine is the fact that you gain a greater grip strength. This is mainly because the kettlebell handle together with the displaced load needs your hands, fingers, and forearms to work together for total control as compared to using a dumbbell.

While so many manufacturers prefer thick handles, one thing that you have to understand is that when you use a narrower handle, you are making it quite easy to perform complex movements. This increases your training options.

Because grip strength is much more significant than in most sports as well as gaining overall strength, kettlebell has the opportunity of boosting your cardiovascular endurance. kettlebell exercises often incorporate the whole body and

workouts as the press, snatch and clean involve lifting weights right from the floor to over the head. This ensures that the muscles across the body are worked well and these motions create a huge demand on the heart. As a result, so many athletes employ the use of kettlebells as a strong pillar of their workout programs.

4. Easy Portability

Just like exercise bands and suspension trainers, kettlebells are quite portable and easy to bring them with you on travel. This is because they will not roll around in your car as dumbbells do. They will not look out of place when you bring them to the beach with you.

Additionally, unlike the dumbbell, you only need one kettlebell for you to have a great workout. This is because, with just a single kettlebell, you can engage in a large number of exercises, unlike the dumbbell that you mostly need at least a few selections of them to do your regular workouts.

If you intend on working the entire body, you can choose to bring two kettlebells. The truth is, if you have a single kettlebell at the

corner of your room or the back of your car, you pretty much have a portable gym.

5. Lowers Body Fats

So many people desire to shed off a few pounds and hence weight loss is one of their major fitness goals. The good thing with kettlebell training is that you can achieve this easily. The main reason for this is the fact that kettlebell training integrates a large number of high-intensity workouts that allow the body to burn as much fat as possible.

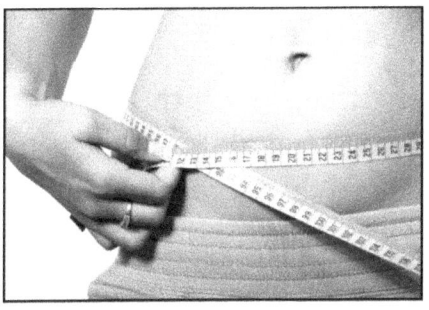

While so many weight loss programs take too much time and effort to achieve the desired body weight and physique and end up becoming boring overtime, kettlebell training is quite the opposite. This is mainly because it serves as an exciting alternative to your average routine workouts because they keep you focused and boost your metabolism rate.

It is highly recommended that if you intend to lose weight using kettlebell training, you integrate a high repetition compound movement exercises in every session. Some of these exercises may include reverse lunges, kettlebell swings and shoulder presses. The most important thing is to ensure that you do not have rest times in between.

6. Improves Posture

One of the things with the human body is that as we age, our posture gets compromised. However, the good thing is that you can make sure that you control the effects of aging by incorporating kettlebell training into your workout routine. This is because, according to research, there is evidence that kettlebell

exercises can improve posture and counter the effects of modern-day lifestyles.

While working out, it is very common for postural muscles to be neglected. But with kettlebell training, you can see results faster and improve your posture. Do you know why this is important? Well, an improved posture helps you look leaner and boosts your self-esteem and confidence.

7. Inexpensive

Kettlebells are cost effective. When you buy the right kettlebell, you can be sure that they will last a lifetime and you will not need to incur another cost of replacing them frequently.

For most beginners, getting a single kettlebell that is made from solid metal can last so many years. Moreover, kettlebell training does not need you to be in specialized footwear like other workouts, and this ensures that you save money that you would have otherwise spent purchasing an expensive pair of workout shoes.

8.Gaining Strength Without Bulk

Did you know that most women who work out possess a common desire to build their strength without necessarily having a bulky appearance of a male bodybuilder? Well, with kettlebell training, the main aim is not to increase the muscle mass but to boost strength without having that bulky appearance.

This is mainly because when you integrate the kettlebell exercises to your training program, you are essentially incorporating full body functional movements. These movements play a central role in simultaneously targeting many muscle groups across the body. If you have any special needs, it is advisable that you speak to your trainer so that they can design workout routines that satisfactorily meet these requirements.

9. Comfortable To Use

Unlike the dumbbells that have a high chance of straining your arms and other workouts that put you at risk of injuries, kettlebells are very comfortable to use. This is mainly because they do not pull the muscles across the body too hard. Their weights rest comfortably in your forearms without weighing them down and causing fatigue. This explains why women prefer using kettlebells than other weight lifting exercises available.

10. Quick Workout

Most of us do not have enough time to sign up and hit the gym. However, this does not mean that there are no workout exercises that will help you keep your great body in shape. Kettlebell exercises are perfect for you, and you can do them at the comfort of your home, office or any other place that you are comfortable with.

Kettlebells target so many muscles in the body, and this means that you do not have to spend so much time on other workouts that only target one body part at a time. This is exactly what makes kettlebell trainings a brilliant solution for people who have busy schedules like moms. Best of all, you can perform these workout exercises with minimal supervision.

Chapter 5: Kettlebell Training

Kettlebells are strength training equipments that have been raved about for a few years. Kettlebells are iron balls that range from 5 to 100 pounds. Kettlebells originated in Russia and have started to gain popularity in the USA.

Kettlebells offer a different type of workout since it targets almost every muscle in the body. It can also be used for endurance, balance, agility and strength cardio training.

The main idea of kettlebell training is to hold it with one hand or both hands while going through a series of movements like swings, pulling motions or presses. Some exercises require you to shift the weight as you move. This allows you to engage your core better.

Difference with dumbbells

Most people may associate kettlebells with dumbbells. The main difference between dumbbells and kettlebells is the shape. The handle of the kettlebell has a different effect on the body.

When you use dumbbells, the weight rests on your hand, when using kettlebells, the weight is transferred outside the hand which means that it can change depending on your movement. Many kettlebell exercises focus on centrifugal force which distributes the weight to the muscles. These types of movements mimic real life activities. Dumbbells are great for building muscles using controlled movements while kettlebells are used for whole body workouts using dynamic movements.

Benefits of kettlebell training

- It combines cardio and strength training. Kettlebell training is similar to running while carrying a heavy load.

- Burns more fat. Kettlebell exercises use explosive movements that make use of muscle groups and increases the metabolic load of the body.

- Kettlebells exercises can improve your agility and coordination.

- It improves alignment muscles which results in better posture.

- It is time efficient. Kettlebell exercises enable you to train multiple components of your body.

- Help you become more efficient in other types of exercise.

- Improves stamina and endurance.

- It can help people avoid injuries. Kettlebell trains you in eccentric deceleration which can strengthen the body.

- Simplicity. The equipment is easy to handle and most exercises are straightforward.

- Time efficient. People who may not have enough time to go to the gym can choose to perform a few minutes of kettlebell exercise for a complete body workout.

- Calorie burning capabilities. On average, people can burn as much as 1,200 calories in an hour while performing kettlebell exercises.

Kettlebell safety

Just like any other exercise, people have to take the necessary precaution when handling kettlebells. Using kettlebells require strength, coordination and practice. It is important to start your workout slow and build the pace as you progress. Avoid lifting heavy kettlebells if you are a beginner since this can result in multiple injuries.

Basic kettlebell movements

Dead lift

Many kettlebell exercises use dead lift movements. Dead lift is good for relaxing hip reflectors as well as strengthening the quad muscles. It is a good idea to master this basic step since it is the foundation of other movements.

Stand with your feet slightly apart. Turn your toes slightly outward. Position yourself as if you are going to sit in a chair. Keep your heels on the ground. Pick up the kettlebell using both of your hands. Make sure to keep your arms straight. Lift the kettlebell until your legs are straight. Do not bend your arms and never place pressure on your back. Your body should form a straight line when you are standing. Lower the kettlebell and repeat the movement.

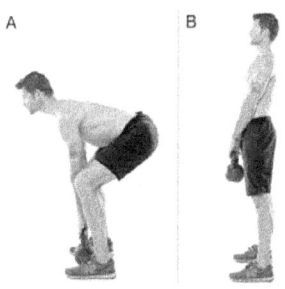

Swing

Two-arm swing is always used in kettlebell training. It is considered as a full body exercise and can be used to increase the explosiveness of dead lifts and squat.

Stand with your feet apart. Place the weight between your heels. Lower your body and grab the handle of the kettlebell with both of your hands. Your arms should be straight with your shoulders back. Your weight should be placed at your heels and not your toes.

Push your hips towards the kettlebell and swing it in front of you. Allow the kettlebell to swing back behind your butt. Once the bell is below your butt, drive your hips forward and swing it until the bell reaches your chest level. Let your arms swing back until the kettlebell swings behind you. Remember to keep your head up and your back straight.

Clean and press

Clean and press is a basic kettlebell step that requires full body movement. Start by straddling the kettlebell. Keep your feet shoulder-width apart. Squat and hold the handle with one hand using the overhand grip. Position your shoulder over the kettlebell while keeping your back straight.

1. Pull the kettlebell off the floor and push your hips forward.

2. When the kettlebell is off the ground, pull it over your shoulder and allow your elbow to bend to the side.

3. Once the kettlebell is positioned in front of your chest, rotate your elbow under the bell.

4. Catch the kettlebell using the outside of your arm. Keep your wrist straight and your knees bent. This may also be called as the rack position.

5. Press the kettlebell off your arm and lockout over your head.

6. Lower the kettlebell and return to the rack position. Lower the kettlebell to the ground and repeat the movement.

Getup

Getup is considered as one of the simple yet physically challenging kettlebell exercise. It engages the whole body and helps in improving stability and balance. It is highly recommended to use a lighter kettlebell in performing the getup for beginners.

1. Lie down with the kettlebell to your side. Hold the kettlebell in your right hand and extend it to your chest level.

2. Bend your right leg and make sure that your heel is placed near your butt. Keep your left leg straight and place your left arm to the side. Your right arm should be fully extended above your head. Push your chest out.

3. Lift your right shoulder and use your left elbow for support. Keep the kettlebell above your head.

4. Transition from the left elbow to the right hand. Keep your right arm fully extended.

5. Push your hips upward and squeeze your glutes.

6. Sweep your left leg behind you so that your left knee is facing the ground. This is also called as the lunge position. Stand up, keep your arms straight.

Chapter 6: Russian Kettlebell Swing

This is a classic Kettlebell movement and is perfect for beginners.

Muscles targeted: Hips, Legs, Glutes, Back, Shoulders

Method:

Stand with your feet shoulder width apart, stand straight and keep your neck in a neutral position. Take the kettlebell handle in both hands while keeping your arms in front of you and your palms facing the floor. Bend your knees slightly lowering your body to the ground while driving your hips backwards. Do not go too low; this should be half way between a squat and a stand. Count to three in your head and then fluidly explode upwards, driving your hips forward. Contract your abs and glutes for stability. You should swing the kettlebell out in front of you until your arms are parallel to the floor. This is a movement that comes from a hip drive rather then from the arms. Work with the motion of the swing and once you have reached the point where your arms are parallel to the floor, lower the kettlebell back down to the starting position. This movement should be as fluid as possible with no rests in between reps. Once you have returned the kettlebell to the starting position, commence the next rep. The important thing about this movement is to work with the swinging motion rather then against it.

Video: https://www.youtube.com/watch?v=uUpSFguwRQM

Single Arm Kettlebell swing

This is similar to the Russian kettlebell swing but is done unilaterally.

Alternate the arm between sets.

Muscle targeted: Hips, Legs, Glutes, Back, Shoulders

Method:

The starting position for this movement is the same as the Russian Kettlebell swing. You should stand straight with your feet shoulder width apart, keeping your neck in a neutral position. Take the kettlebell handle in one hand keeping the other hand free to swing and drive momentum. Bend your knees slightly lowering your body to the ground while driving your hips backwards. Do not go too low; this should be half way between a squat and a stand. Explode upwards, driving your hips forward. Contract your abs and glutes for stability. You should swing the kettlebell out in front of you until your arm is parallel to the floor. Simultaneously swing out your free arm to aid momentum. This is a movement that comes from a hip drive rather then from the arms so try not to lock out your arms. Similarly to the Russian swing, remember to work with the motion of the swing and once you have reached the point where your arms are parallel to the floor, lower the kettlebell back down to the starting position. The important thing about this movement is to work with the swinging motion rather then against it. Don't switch arms between each rep, wait until the end of the set. This should allow you to work the muscles in each arm to their full potential.

Video: https://www.youtube.com/watch?v=R8uI-EopErw

One Arm Kettlebell clean

This is a really great movement for engaging the back and legs; it can take some time to get the hang of, so take it slow to begin with.

Muscles targeted: Back, Legs, Glutes, Core

Method:

Start with your legs shoulder width apart. Place the kettlebell between your feet. Take the kettlebell in one hand with a loose grip with your thumb pointed behind you (this should prevent the kettlebell hitting your wrists). Shrug the shoulders and pull the bell up to shoulder level (into rack position). While pulling the kettlebell upwards you should exhale and tense the muscles in your core and glutes. You should aim to keep the kettlebell close to your body at all times. Keep the arm not lifting the kettlebell tight at all times, refrain from swinging it as you move upwards. Visualize the kettlebell going straight up from the floor. At the top of the rep, the Kettlebell should be resting on the forearm with your fist touching your chest. In a slow and controlled motion, reverse the motion and bring the kettlebell back to its starting position. Refrain from switching arms between reps, swap between sets instead.

Video: https://www.youtube.com/watch?v=6AIlgwod8cY

Top Tips:

- Remember to keep that grip loose

- It's really important to engage your core at the top of the movement.

- Don't forget to swap arms between sets!

Chapter 7: Combo Exercises (Upper And Lower Body)

Single Arm Kettlebell Swing **– 4 rounds x Max reps**

− Start by standing with your feet wider than shoulder width apart. Hold a kettlebell between your legs with one hand.

− Bend your knees and keep your lower back straight to squat down, gripping the kettlebell tight with your working hand.

− Use your hips and thighs, swing the kettlebell back to create momentum.

− Forcefully reverse the position and swing the kettlebell up and forward using your arm, shoulder, hips, and thighs up to chest or eye level. This constitutes one rep.

− Let the kettlebell swing back down between your legs and perform between 8 to 12 reps per set per arm.

Kettlebell Burpees (Thighs and Core)

- Perform the beginning part of a regular burpee while holding a kettlebell with each hand, keeping your core muscles (abs, lower back) super tight.

- For the second half of the burpee, thrust yourself back up to a standing position, with your lower back straight all throughout, and your head up to complete 1 deadlift rep. This constitutes 1 rep.

- For the second half of the movement, ensure that your feet land between the kettlebells to optimize proper deadlifting form. If you're not yet fit enough to thrust yourself to a standing position, then simply position your feet between the kettlebells prior to executing the deadlift.

- Perform 8 to 12 reps per set.

Chapter 8: High Intensity Interval Training

Because we are following CrossFit principles in our training regimen, we must learn how to execute the High Intensity Interval Training properly. A typical CrossFit session lasts from 30 minutes to 1 hour. You can achieve results even with just a small duration of workout each day because of the use of HIIT.

As the name suggests this type of training uses the interval training method where in workout moves that release strong bursts of energy is followed by a very short period of rest before going to another high intensity workout move.

Using the HIIT, you can choose to focus on one muscle group for the day or to target multiple muscle groups. Your choice should depend in your goals. People who want to build muscles target one muscle group on each workout day to maximize muscle hypertrophy. The HIIT will work their muscles out to the point of exhaustion. After working it out, the muscle group will be allowed to rest for 2 days to allow the muscles to load itself up with protein. This will result to muscle growth and toning.

If you want a slender and toned body on the other hand, you should target multiple body parts on each workout day. This will lessen the chances of injury caused by repetitive use of a muscle. This type of HIIT will also increase your metabolic rate better compared to isolating one muscle group for each workout session.

How to start using HIIT

As with starting any new workout on your own, you should approach HIIT slowly as a beginner. The high intensity workouts are designed to boost the workout performance of athletes. If you are not confident with your athleticism yet, you could start out with short durations of high intensity exercises with resting time double or triple the sprint time.

20 seconds/60 seconds interval

You could start with these durations. The 20 seconds refer to the duration of your high intensity workout and 60 seconds refer to the duration of the resting state that follows.

For example, you could start by doing as many kettlebell snatches for 20 seconds. After that, you should rest for a minute. You should move on to the next workout move for another 20/60 seconds interval.

Chapter 9: Preparing For Your Kettlebell Workout

Weight

What weight should you use or buy?

First of all, its recommended trying out a few exercises in the gym before you buy your own at home. The only one will not be enough for all exercises, but at least you can integrate 2-3 exercises into your training. And if you try it before you know

a) Which exercise you would like to integrate and is suitable for you and your training and

b) What weight you need for it. For example, the Kettlebell Swing is an effective and relatively simple exercise that can be performed with a kettlebell and can be integrated into almost any workout plan.

If you realize Kettlebell training is your thing, it's recommended you buy 3

Kettlebells at different levels. For example, you can have 4-6-10kg at home and get on with it quite well. But that depends on where your current training level is.

Buy a 6kg kettlebell for a while now and just recently ordered two more kettlebells in the online shop Gorilla Sports and so far I'm very satisfied. The handle has a good shape and size, so it feels great in hand. They look very high quality but are still inexpensive.

4kg - 10,90 EUR

6kg - 16,90 EUR 10kg -

18,90 EUR

Technique

A flawless technique is essential for your kettlebell workout. Before you start the training for the first time, you should take a quick look at and practice all the exercises before starting the right workout. Look at yourself in the mirror that helps you to get the right execution.

Without the correct technique, injuries, imbalances, or overloading can occur.

15min kettlebell workout

And now for the most exciting part of the article - a 15min kettlebell workout, the following 15min workout is, as the name implies, short of performing with little space and effective for muscle growth and fat loss. It consists of only two exercises. Both address the entire body and bring the pulse higher to boost metabolism. The maximum effect in no time - what more could you want?

The workout works as follows:

12 x exercise 1

12 x exercise 2

30s rest

11 x exercise 1

11 x exercise 2

30s rest and so on

It is an ideal complement to your training plan. The short amount of time you can put it before work, in the evening after work to switch off or weekend (in the park - if you want to carry your kettlebell there) in addition to do some other exercises.

So and now go to the bacon.

Chapter 10: The 8 Week Training Plan

So begins the 8 week training plan! Enjoy the training time and focus on each movement – make your training as conscious as possible.

If you are new, start with smaller weights and build over the course of the 8 weeks. Make sure to study good sources for movement demos and check your own movements to make sure you are working in a safe manner.

Each week will consist of strength, conditioning, power endurance and some weeks include a flow. I wrote out 4 complete workouts per week. You can supplement these days with other training – running, rowing, powerlifting, gymnastics, kickboxing or jujitsu – or build your own workouts with the bonus workouts in Chapter 9.

Training Terminology

Over the course of the training plan you will come across some of the terms below. Refer back to this list as needed.

AMRAP – "as many rounds (and reps) as possible". In an AMRAP workout, you will work as hard as you can against the clock counting down and attempt to complete as much work as possible in that time.

EMOM – "every minute on the minute". In an EMOM workout, you will begin a new set of work at the start of each minute and use the remaining time within the minute to rest.

For Time – A "for time" conditioning workout means completing the workout as quickly as possible.

Rounds – Rounds in a workout means repeating the sequence of movements for the set amount of rounds. For example, a "5 rounds" workout is complete when all movements within each round are completed 5 times.

Rep scheme – This book follows a sets x reps scheme. This means a 4 x 6 workout would be 4 sets of 6 reps. A workout that looks like "10, 10, 8, 8, 6, 6" would do that many reps with rest in-between. The higher rep sets would be less weight than the lower rep sets.

Week 1

This first week will consist of simple movements and power development. This will form the basis for the 8 week program. Make sure to pay attention the rep scheme and start with smaller weights as you build over the course of the strength work. This week will have a little bit of everything so that you get comfortable with the different types of workouts we will do.

Day 1

Strength:

Goblet squat

10, 10, 10, 8, 8, 8, 6, 6, 6

Farmers carry

1 minute on, 1 minute off for 10 minutes

Conditioning:

75 kettlebell swings

30 burpees

75 kettlebell swings

Day 2

Strength:

Single KB dl

5 x 8

Then:

Turkish get up:

5 x 3L/3R

Power Endurance:

Front racked double kettlebell walking lunges 100 meters and back

*Rest and repeat

Day 3

Strength:

Double kettlebell press

10, 10, 8, 8, 4, 4, 2, 2

Conditioning:

Flow 1

Two kettlebells on floor

Hike to clean

Double front squat

Thruster back to front rack

Reverse lunge each side

Drop kettlebells to floor

Renegade row

Repeat 3x

This completes 1 round, take a short break and repeat 5 times

Day 4

Strength:

Hike to clean

6 x 4l/4r

Conditioning:

4 rounds:

200m farmers carry

1 minute bar hang

20 air squats

Rest 1 minute

Week 2

Day 1

Strength:

Double kettlebell squat

5 x 10

15 push-ups between each round

Conditioning:

3 minutes:

5 goblet squats

10 push up

1 minute rest

3 minutes:

10 kettlebell swings

30 double unders (50 single unders)

1 minute rest

*Repeat whole sequence 1 time for a total of 16 minutes of work.

Day 2

Strength:

Single leg kettlebell DL

5 x 10

EMOM for 10 minutes

15-20 kettlebell swings

Conditioning:

4 rounds for time

10 goblet squats

5 right side overhead press

10 goblet squat

5 left side overhead press

15 push up

Day 3

Strength:

Double KB press

5x6

Then:

Accumulate 20 alternating Turkish get-ups at low to medium weight

Conditioning:

10 rounds

50 jump rope

10 push-up

10 goblet or mace squat

Day 4

Strength:

Snatch complex:

Snatch 3 times on right side from a swing

3 right side swings

Transition to left

3 left side snatch from a swing

3 swing

Then:

5 rounds:

10 alternating kettlebell figure 8

Conditioning:

50 kb swings

200 jump rope

30 burpees

100 jump rope

15 pull ups

50 jump rope

Week 3

Week 3 starts with Turkish get-ups and windmills. These are complex and multi-skilled movements, so work slowly and with lighter weight if this is the first time you have done these movements. We will end this week with a classic Tabata protocol workout. Give it your all and really push it!

Day 1

Strength:

Turkish get-up

4 x 3r/3l

*use a heavier weight than last week

Then:

Kettlebell windmill

3 x 5l/5r

Power endurance:

Repeat 50m farmers carry for 20 minutes. Rest as needed.

Day 2

Strength:

Double KB squat

5 x 8

Then:

6 rounds:

8l/8r kettlebell row

15 push ups

Rest as needed between sets

Then:

6 rounds:

10 weighted step-ups

10 kettlebell swings

Day 3

Strength:

Seesaw press

6 x 8

Then:

Floor press

5 x 5

Conditioning:

Flow 2:

1l kettlebell hike clean

3l swing cleans

3l overhead press

1r kettlebell hike clean

3r swing cleans

3r overhead press

Rest :30 seconds and repeat 10 times

Day 4

Strength:

Single kettlebell snatch

Build weight progressively over sets:

8 x 5l/5r

Then:

5 sets of ME weighted pull-ups

*ME = Max Effort – max effort means to perform as many reps as possibly per set until you can no longer continue.

Conditioning:

:20 on/ :10 off

Squat

Squat

Swing

Swing

Clean and press

Clean and press

Deadlift

Week 4

This week will incorporate a lot of single kettlebell work. Use this as an opportunity for conscious training and building functional stability.

The squat complex will have you perform 3 single sided front squats and then moving the kettlebell to your back to complete 3 back squats then switch sides.

Day 1

Strength:

Single arm deadlift

6 x 4l/4r

*use a heavy weight and focus on stability

Power endurance:

2 mile run

400m sandbag carry

30 burpees

30 pull-ups

200m kettlebell farmers carry

30 squats

30 push-ups

2 mile run

Day 2

Strength:

Single kb squat complex

Perform 8 sets of:

3r front squat

3r back squat

3l front squat

3l back squat

Then:

5 x 5 sandbag clean and press

Conditioning:

Flow 3:

Start in hike position

Double kb swing

Double kb clean and press

KB drop to floor

Sprawl off kettlebell

Double KB deadlift

2 Push-up off KB handle

Renegade row right/left

Return to hike position

Perform 2 times through, rest and repeat entire flow 6 times

Day 3

Strength:

Single arm overhead press

6 x 4l/4r

Conditioning:

12 minute EMOM

15 KB swings

15 sit ups

15 ring dips

*if you do not have access to rings, perform normal dips; if you don't have the

ability to do bar dips, substitute 20 push-ups

Power endurance:

10 minutes AMRAP

50m sled drag

Day 4

Strength:

Single kb clean

Accumulate as many quality reps as possible in 10 minutes of the pattern

3 left, swing to change hands, 3 right.

Conditioning:

8 rounds

10 kb deadlifts

15 pull-ups

20 push-ups

Week 5

Day 1

Strength:

Double overhead kettlebell squat

10, 10, 8, 8, 5, 5, 5

*Perform 10 push-ups and 10 chin-ups between sets

Conditioning:

4 rounds:

200 meter farmers carry

10 sandbag clean

10 burpee

1 minute bar hang

Day 2

Strength:

6 rounds:

6 double swing

4 double snatch

Then:

Weighted lunges

5 x 12

Conditioning:

8 minute EMOM:

15 Kettlebell swing

Day 3

Strength:

Clean and press

5, 5, 5, 3, 3, 3, 1, 1

Then:

Floor press

5 x 10

Then:

Weighted step-ups

6 x 20

Day 4

Strength:

Kettlebell windmill

6 x 3l/3r

Conditioning:

1 minute on each exercise:

Kettlebell 2 hand row
Double kettlebell clean to squat
Sandbag shouldering
Pull-ups
Abmat sit-ups

*Rest 1 minute and repeat for a total of 5 sets

Week 6

We have another new movement this week, the single press with farmers hold. For this movement, hold one kettlebell in a farmers carry position while pressing the other kettlebell overhead from a front rack position. We also have some power endurance training with AMRAP sled drags.

Day 1

Strength:

6 rounds:

10 goblet squat

*10 push-up and 5 chin-up between strength rounds

Conditioning:

3 rounds:

Run 400 meters

21 kettlebell swings

12 pull-ups

Day 2

Strength:

Double KB deadlift

8, 8, 8, 6, 6, 6

Then:

Romanian deadlift

4x8

Conditioning:

Flow 3:

Start in hike position

Double kb swing

Double kb clean and press

KB drop to floor

Sprawl off kettlebell

Double KB deadlift

2 Push-up off KB handle

Renegade row right/left

Return to hike position

Complete this flow 2 times through and complete the entire flow sequence for 6 times total.

Day 3

Strength:

Single arm press, farmers

6x6

Conditioning:

5 rounds, work 30 seconds, rest 30 seconds:

Kettlebell swings

Ball slams

Sit ups

Walking lunges (weighted if you desire)

Day 4

Strength:

Weighted step-ups

5 x 10l/10r

Then:

Weighted pull up

5 x ME

*ME = Max Effort – max effort means to perform as many reps as possibly per set until you can no longer continue.

Power endurance:

20 minute AMRAP

Sled drag

10 burpees at the start of every 2 minutes

Week 7

Day 1

Strength:

10 rounds:

5 double KB squat to 5 thruster

*90 second rest between sets

Flow:

Flow 1:

Two kettlebells on floor

Hike to clean

Double front squat

Thruster back to front rack

Reverse lunge each side

Drop kettlebells to floor

Renegade row

Repeat 3x

This completes 1 round, take a short break and repeat 5 times

Day 2

Strength:

6 rounds:

With 2 kettlebells,

1 Hike clean to 2 swing clean

5 thruster

Conditioning:

4 rounds:

15 goblet squat

200m farmer carries

Day 3

Strength:

10 rounds:

2L, 2R Kettlebell clean + push press

4 Pull-up

:20 sec. rest

Then:

See-saw press

5x5l/5r

Conditioning:

45 seconds of work/1 minute rest

Kettlebell swing

Push-up

Day 4

Strength:

8 rounds:

10 Floor press

5 dips

5 chin-up

Conditioning:

21-15-9-15-21:

Ball slam

Jump squat

Sit-up

*30 jump rope between rounds

Week 8

Our last week! Keep the intensity.

Day 1

Strength:

Goblet squat

5 x 8

Then:

Front rack double kettlebell walking lunge

4 x 20

Conditioning:

Alternating EMOM for 10 minutes

Even minutes:

20 swings

Odd minutes:

15 burpees

Day 2

Strength:

Single leg dl

8 x 6l/6r

Conditioning:

10 minute AMRAP

10 deadlifts

400m run

Day 3

Strength:

8 rounds:

3r snatch

3r press

3l snatch

3l press

Then:

Weighted step-ups

5 x 20

Conditioning:

2 times through:

3 minute AMRAP:

5 goblet squat

10 push-ups

Rest 1:00, then

3 minute AMRAP:

10 kettlebell swings

60 jump rope

Rest 1:00

Day 4

Strength:

8 rounds:

4l/4r row

4l/4r floor press

Then:

8 minute EMOM:

15 kettlebell swings

Conditioning:

Flow 2:

Single kettlebell on floor

Hike to swing

Swing to clean

Clean to overhead press

Overhead press to squat to thruster

Swing to hand change

Repeat on other side

Rest and repeat for total reps for 10 minutes

Checking in

So how do you feel?

Hopefully, after these 8 weeks of training, you're feeling strong and ready to tackle new challenges with strength and fitness. If you did the conditioning side, you should also feel new levels of aerobic fitness.

Use movements such as the goblet squat and single kettlebell deadlift to test and retest your strength numbers as you continue. See how heavy you can go and track progress over time. Return to workouts in this guide too and see how much easier and quicker you can complete them.

Chapter 11: Rules For Structuring Workouts

Each session **must** have **one** of the three essential movements

Kettlebell Swings

Turkish Getups

Squat and Press

Note: I generally use the kettlebell swing as a conclusion to the workout. Turkish getups tie in well with a chest or back workout day as they are less taxing than the other two exercises on your legs.

Workout Frequency

This is really down to your personal goals; a minimum of two 30minute workouts that concentrate on compound moves can be effective. The sweet spot for me personally is around the 3-4 sessions per week with each session having a focus given to legs, back or chest (I never separate abs as it should in incorporated into every session by default due to the compound nature of the movements.)

If you are going for minimalist training and what to achieve the most with the least:

Day 1:

KB Squat and Press 4 sets x 15 reps

KB Swing 3 sets x 30 reps

Burpees 1 set x 50 reps

Day 2

KB Turkish Getups 3 sets x 10 reps

KB Renegade Row (with push up)   3 sets x 15 reps

Pull-ups   3 sets x max reps

A template of a 4 workout week is given below (generally what I adhere to.)

Monday: Legs

KB Squat and Press 4 sets x 15 reps

KB Lunges 3 sets x 20 reps (10 per side)

KB Swing 3 sets x 30 reps

Tuesday: Chest

KB swissball Press 3 sets x 15 reps

KB Turkish Getups 3 sets x 10 reps

Tricep Dips 3 sets x 15 reps

Wednesday: Back

KB Renegade Row 3 sets 15 reps

Pull-ups   3 sets x max reps

KB Swing 3 x 30 reps

Thursday: KB Cardio

KB snatchs   1 set x 100 reps

Burpees 1 set x 50 Burpees

Best Time of Day to Train

When you train will generally depend on personal factors such as work, kids, accessibility, etc. I am a strong supporter of early morning workouts if you have the option for the below reasons:

It is a great way to start the day which offers a lasting energy boost throughout the day

You can choose to workout in a fasted state if desire

It doesn't affect sleep patterns like late night workouts can.

An essential element if you do decide you are going to work out in the early hours is a reliable training partner to ensure you do not roll over and hit the snooze on the alarm – you need someone to hold you accountable.

Eating Paleo/Whole Foods

I prefer not to think of this as a diet but rather a conscious decision not to eat the mountains of processed, additive-loaded, preservative-packed junk we find on the shelves of our local supermarkets. If you have to ask the question of whether you can eat something, just ask yourself would a caveman recognise it? Bread, pasta, chips, biscuits - a caveman won't have a clue what these are. You've already probably heard the standard Paleo rules: eat meat, fish, vegetables, fruits and nuts. So I want to propose eating Paleo in a more practical way, essentially with a few simple meals you can eat again and again. As most of us end up eating similar meals anyway (such as a bowl of cereal for breakfast and a sandwich for lunch), the aim is just to replace these with better options. What follows are the meals I've ended up eating approximately 85% of the time over the last few years, they are my default meals.

3 Power Breakfasts

Two boiled eggs and a handful of almonds (great if you're on the run and "don't have time for breakfast".) I boil 12 eggs then put them straight back into the cartoon so I have quick and healthy meals/snacks always on hand.

Poached/scrambled eggs and half an avocado (if I have a long day ahead or know I will be tempted by junk food throughout the day than a larger breakfast with lots of healthy fats is my go to).

Smoothie: Good quality protein powder, a spoonful of peanut butter and handful of berries (I use Sunwarrior protein powder, as it doesn't cause bloating like whey and I don't trust soy.)

Those are your choices, nice and simple. I would also add a cup of green tea or black coffee if you must and at least 500ml of water first thing in the morning.

Supplements that Work

A quality brand of fish oil. Use www.labdoor.com (Comparison website that actually lab tests products to find the superior quality.)

A vitamin D supplement: aim for 5000-10000IU per day which is well above what most supplements contain. Unless you are getting 1hour plus of direct sunlight on your face and a decent amount of your body chances are your vitamin D levels are below optimum, if not deficient.

2 Power Lunch's

Tuna mashed into half an avocado with salad and fresh lemon and cracker pepper. It's a versatile meal and you don't have to have access to a kitchen to prepare it as there's no need to heat or cook anything.

Stir-frys such as chicken and cashew with plenty of vegetables (no rice or sweet sauces). I always make double the portion size when cooking dinner and store the left overs in Tupperware for lunch the next day. Few quick rules for a healthy and tasty stir fry are:

Always cook the meat first in the wok then set to the side.

Next do the vegetables, as this prevents the stir-fry becoming soggy.

Use sesame seed oil, macadamia oil or coconut oil - never olive, canola or vegetable oil.

You don't need sweet sauces, fresh herbs, garlic, ginger, chilli limes and soy sauce is all you will ever need.

The aim is to replace the calories from rice with roasted cashews or peanuts, giving the stir-fry a good crunch, or use satay sauce (see below).

Quick way to make satay sauce: boil water in kettlebell then pour a small amount in the bottom of a coffee cup and place a forkful of peanut butter in the cup and tilt it so the peanut butter is just covered in boiled water which will start to melt it. Continue to whisk the melting peanut butter until it is creamy, then add a splash of soy sauce and you are done. Simple and tasty.

4 Quick Snacks

Mixed raw nuts and an apple or piece of jerky

Spoonful of peanut butter and handful of frozen berries

Boiled egg and handful of mixed raw nuts

Small flavoured cans of tuna (eat directly out of can with a teaspoon.)

These can all be fine for a replacement meal in itself by bumping up the proportion size. For nuts your go-to should be raw almonds (approx. 15 almonds depending on your weight.)

4 Ways to Finish Strong with Dinner

Cook fish or chicken along with a healthy serving of broccoli, asparagus or kale wrapped in aluminium foil with a generous splash of coconut oil or olive oil before putting in the oven for 20-30mins at 200 degrees. Quick, healthy, little to wash up and you don't have to monitor it while it cooks. Can experiment with herbs, limes, garlic which can infuse the food with great flavours while cooking.

Stir fry as mentioned in lunches.

Poaching or steaming fish or chicken is also quick and healthy. Use one of your standard pots along with a steamer basket, then throw everything in put the lid on leave it for 10mins. Plate steamed food and add coconut oil or olive oil along with herbs to give the food some flavour (which steaming can remove).

George foreman: a good non-stick George foreman grill is great from grilling onion and asparagus before putting in seasoned chicken or fish.

Extra Tips to Give You the Edge

Just because it's natural doesn't mean you can eat all the fruit you like. Restrict fruit to directly before and after workouts. This will help ensure all the sugar that hits your blood stream is utilised and doesn't end up being stored (as fat.) The exception to this is berries (blueberries, raspberries, and blackberries), which you can eat whenever suits you (within reason).

As you may have noticed all the above meals are low-carb, the body can operate well utilising fats as its main fuel source (don't be afraid to eat more peanut butter or cover your food in coconut oil) as there is no insulin spike so the body gets a nice even flow of energy, as well as being full for longer. By eating more fat your hunger should start to regulate itself, instead of the blood sugar spike from the sugary breakfast cereal followed by the crash before lunch, just as you are walking past the donut store... The stigma society has around fat is unfounded and I have always wondered if fat were to be renamed energy and better understood, then obesity rates would be slashed.

Actively attempt to avoid cooked food whenever possible, as the more enzymatically alive food you can consume, the better your general gut health will be. Your ability to extract nutrients from the foods you eat does come down to the health of your digestive tract. An interesting little experiment you can undertake to reinforce the above points is to get two seedlings and plant them in two separate pots. Once they are a few centimetres out of the ground you continue watering one with plain tap water. For the other you are to microwave the water first to boiling, then put in the fridge to cool down. Once the waters cooled, use it to water the other seedling. What you will find is the microwaved watered seedling will start to die. If microwaving can change the structure of water to make it unsuitable for plants, what is it doing to humans that studies have yet to pick up on? The easiest way I have found to incorporate a lot more raw food into my diet is via smoothies and eating a lot more raw nuts to fuel myself.

Drink a ton of water! It's really that simple, water to the body is what oil is to a car. Sure, the car can run with less oil but it will cause unnecessary wear on the engine and shorten its lifespan. Dehydration has the same effect on the human body, as kidneys can't function effectively to remove toxins when the body is forced to conserve its fluid levels. A decrease of only a few percent in your body's total fluid levels can seriously impair both mental and physical performance. Always start your day with an internal bath for your body, so drink at least 500ml of cold water within twenty minutes of waking up. Generally we will always wake up in a mild state of dehydration, due to breathing through your mouth while sleeping, air-conditioning or the heating drying you out, or simply because you've just gone 7-9 hours without water.

Drinking alcohol: No one wants to be that person at the party with their hands empty, the one who has to tell every second person that asks why they are not drinking tonight. Wine is fine; just keep it to a maximum of 2-3 glasses. If it's more of a celebration or you simply feel like letting your hair down but want to limit the damage, then vodka and soda with a wedge of lime should be your go-to. Vodka is the easiest of the spirits for the liver to process, while the soda will help keep you hydrated (avoid sugar) and the lime adds a small detoxifying health kick. Lastly, aim to have eaten and digested your food prior to drinking more than 1 or 2 drinks, the reason being that the body treats alcohol like a poison, so it will put all other processes on hold until it has detoxified the body. This means the kebab you just ate on the way home from the party is not going to be properly digested and will likely end up stored as fat.

Cheat days and damage control. Yes we all need to have a blow out and eat two large pizzas or a whole family serving of Chinese occasionally. The trick is to prepare your body in such a way that your insulin is prevented from spiking which results in fat storage. Below are my tips to limit the damage on a day where I know I'm going to be bad.

Consume a large protein and healthy fat rich breakfast to start the day (2-3 eggs and half an avocado will help balance insulin).

Use cinnamon prior to a high GI meal as it has compounds that increase insulin sensitivity to help balance blood sugar.

Almonds prior to a high GI meal can also reduce an insulin spike by up to 50% due to their high fibre content and mono-saturated fats. A small handful of 10-15 should do the trick and be filling enough to help prevent you going completely over board with the pizza.

Having freshly squeezed lemon in water is yet another means to help keep your blood sugar under control.

Weight training prior to a binge can also help ensure the food you eat in the following hours is utilised to feed your muscles and not sit on your belly. It also doesn't have to be proper gym weight lifting either, it can simply be dropping and doing 50 press ups or 50 sit-ups to active Glut-4 (glucose transporter type 4) which opens the gates for calories to flow directly into muscles cells (I highly recommend you read Tim Ferriss's 'Four Hour Body' if you are interested in this, along with a ton of other interesting case studies and experiments).

Finally, drink green tea, as many studies support the way in which it can inhibit the storage of excess carbohydrates as body fat and preferentially direct them into muscle cells. Also doubles as a great pre-workout!

Chapter 12: Personalize It!

Working your way through all three kettlebell training difficulty levels is a great place to start but where do you go from there?

MAKE IT YOUR OWN

Being able to customize your workout by mixing and matching single exercises is a great way to keep your body on its toes and stave off boredom. Being able to create your own workout plan allows you to choose exercises you enjoy and target areas you want to develop.

CHOOSE A FOCUS

When setting up your own, personalized kettlebell workout, you first need to decide what you want to focus on and achieve from that workout. There are four possible areas of focus:

Upper body

Lower body

Core

Full-body

You can design a number of workouts based on different areas of focus for different days of the week.

EXERCISE SELECTION

The exercises you choose will be dictated by your area of focus and goals. Many kettlebell moves will work multiple muscle groups throughout your body in a single exercise. However, most exercises will have a main focus. Use the handy variety of exercises provided under each category in the workout chapters to select exercises based on the focus of your particular workout plan.

When putting together a full-body workout plan, you aren't restricted to moves like the kettlebell swing which are labeled as 'full-body.' You can, and should, consider choosing exercises that fall under the upper body, lower body, and core and mixing them up in a workout to achieve an all-in-one workout plan.

STRENGTH VS CARDIO

Another consideration when choosing a focus for your workout plan is to decide whether you want to train for increased strength or cardio.

A strength-based plan will see you performing slower and using a much heavier weight. For strength development, you need to choose a weight that you can only lift for about 10 repetitions of a move before you are maxed out. This means that you will really be pushing your muscles to make it through a workout and your workouts will be shorter with a lower number of repetitions.

A cardio-focused plan will include moves that provide good cardio without increasing the weight by much. Lighter weight and faster movements will get your heart racing and allow you to train for a longer period of time without muscle fatigue.

REPETITIONS VS INTERVALS

Each workout can be classed as a repetition-based workout or an interval-based workout. A repetition-based workout would be based on a predetermined number of repetitions and sets for each exercise. An interval-based workout will be based on performing each exercise for a certain amount of time before moving on to the next exercise.

Often repetition-based plans are useful for strength training while interval-based plans are better suited for cardio but there is a lot of scope to play around when creating your own workouts.

EXERCISE ORDER

The order in which you place your chosen kettlebell exercises within your workout plan is almost as important as the exercises you choose. Clumping similar exercises together that work the same parts of your body in succession can cause muscle fatigue and overuse. Ideally, you should alternate upper body, core, and lower body moves to give each area a rest between exercises that target them while you are working on another area.

THE REPETITION PLAN

When building a repetition-based workout plan, you need to decide what outcome you want:

Muscle endurance

Muscle size

Muscle strength and power

Your goal will determine the number of repetitions, sets, and resting time between sets.

Muscle Endurance:

Build muscle to perform more reps for longer without tiring

Light weight

High reps: 12 – 20+

Sets: 3 – 5

Less rest: 30 – 60 seconds or up to 1 – 2 minutes between sets

Muscle Size:

Build bigger muscles.

Heavy weight

Medium reps: 6 – 12

Sets: 3 – 5

More rest: 60 – 90 seconds or up to 2 – 3 minutes between sets

Strength and Power:

Build muscle that is stronger but not necessarily bigger

Very heavy weight

Low reps: 1 – 5

Sets: 3 – 5

Long rest: up to 3 – 5 minutes between sets

THE INTERVAL PLAN

When you are creating an interval workout plan, you are going to be designating active phases and resting phases. Active phases refer to the time spent performing the exercise while resting phases refer to the rest time between active phases.

As a rule of thumb, active phases should range from 30 seconds to two minutes while resting phases should range from 10 seconds to 30 seconds. How long your active and resting phases are will be determined by your level of conditioning. Before you put an interval plan together, test yourself out to see how long you can comfortably perform an exercise for and how long it takes you to recover after the active phase. Using that information, you can tailor your interval workout to your own needs.

HOW MANY EXERCISES

It can be tricky to decide which kettlebell exercises to include in your workout but there is a guideline on how many you should include per plan. Kettlebells work out large numbers of muscles during each exercise. This means that you should include fewer exercises per workout than if you were focusing on single or smaller muscle groups in each plan. Ideally, you should try to pick three to four exercises each for the upper body, lower body, and core to facilitate a successful full-body workout.

CHOOSING A WEIGHT

Choosing a weight for your workout plan will depend on your goals and your capabilities. It is also a matter of trial and error. It is best to err on the side of caution and always start with a weight that is lighter than you think you can handle. It's better to realize you could have done more reps or used a heavier weight than to finish a workout and have to call an ambulance to take you to hospital.

For repetition-based workouts start with a lighter weight and perform the lower number of reps and sets recommended. Once you have completed the workout, assess how you feel and plan to either increase the weight or the number of reps and sets, until you find your balance between weight and reps/sets.

For interval-based workouts start with a lighter weight and intervals that have shorter active phases and longer rest phases. After you have completed your first workout, you can reassess whether you need to increase the weight or increase the active phases and decrease the rest phases.

Only through experimenting with the variables and learning to listen to your body will you be able to work out the kinks and develop a workout plan that is perfect for your needs.

WHEN TO INCREASE WEIGHT OR REPS/SETS

There is no hard and fast rule about increasing the weight of your kettlebell or the number of repetitions or sets you are performing. This is a personal choice and you need to really listen to your body when you are trying to decide on upping the ante.

REPS AND SETS

Kettlebell weight increases make big jumps so it can be intimidating to make the decision to increase the weight. It can often be easier to first increase the number of repetitions and sets before making the big leap of upping the weight. Here's how to do it.

When using the beginner, intermediate, and advanced workouts detailed in earlier chapters, progress your workouts as follows:

Start off with the recommended weight as outlined in Chapter 3. Start with the lowest number of reps and sets recommended. In this case it would be eight reps for three sets. As you become more comfortable, increase your reps by one per set to nine reps for three sets. Continue increasing the reps until you have reached the maximum recommended number of reps per set. Then begin increasing the number of sets.

If you find it difficult to increase the sets at the maximum recommended reps, lower the reps back to eight and increase the sets instead, once you have reached the maximum recommended number of sets, begin increasing the reps per set.

Once you can comfortably perform five sets of 10 reps each, it's time to reconsider increasing the weight or training for endurance.

WEIGHT

Kettlebell weight increases can be quite large compared to the smaller incremental increases available with traditional weight lifting such as dumbbells. Weight plates for dumbbells and barbells come in sizes as small as 500 g/1lb. Kettlebells, on the other hand, typically offer increases of 4 kg/9 lbs at a jump. This being said, the decision to upgrade your kettlebell to a heavier one shouldn't be taken lightly.

Before you increase the weight, you should have perfected the form. Once you have perfected your form, your decision will be further influenced by your muscle-building goal.

If you want to build muscle endurance, you may want to consider increasing weight after you can perform seamless sets consisting of upwards of 20+ reps for the maximum number of sets of an exercise such as a press or kettlebell swing. Each repetition should be smooth and perfectly executed and you shouldn't feel tired by the end of a set.

If you want to build muscle bulk or size, you may want to consider increasing the weight of your kettlebell when you can perform 6 - 12 repetitions per set for the maximum number of sets without becoming fatigued or compromising form.

For building power and strength, you might want to consider increasing your kettlebell weight when you can perform 3 - 5 repetitions of an exercise per set for the maximum number of sets without tiring.

If you are uncertain at all about increasing your weight, it's a good idea to seek advice from a trainer. Due to the large increases in weight as you upgrade from one kettlebell to the next heaviest option, the risk of injury is always there. You don't even have to go into a gym to speak to a trainer, there are lots of forums available where personal trainers frequently offer their advice to fitness newbies. Many trainers and instructors also have their own websites through which you can contact them. Just remember the rule of thumb; when in doubt, reach out.

Conclusion

Now you know how to Supercharge your workout to lose fat and get into great shape fast in as little time possible. Give the workout in this book a try for a month or so and I guarantee you'll see better results than if you were to do the traditional long, slow cardio workouts using fitness equipment at your gym. You'll lose belly fat, build a bit of lean muscle, look better, and have more fun too.

Remember that diet is important too. By cutting back on carbohydrates or following a high protein diet (such as the Paleo Diet) you'll see results even faster.

www.ingramcontent.com/pod-product-compliance
Lightning Source LLC
LaVergne TN
LVHW011956070526
838202LV00054B/4940